For Your Garden

FOUNTAINS AND
CASCADES

For Your Garden

FOUNTAINS AND CASCADES

Teri Dunn

FRIEDMAN/FAIRFAX

PUBLISHERS

DEDICATION

For Shawn, Wes, and Tris, with love.
Thanks for inspiration: Ursula K. LeGuin's story "The Fountains," published in a collection called *Orsinian Tales*; the Crystal Springs Rhododendron Garden's fountains (Portland, Oregon); and the many fountains of Santa Barbara, from State Street to the Old Mission.

A FRIEDMAN/FAIRFAX BOOK

Library of Congress Cataloging-in-Publication Data available upon request

ISBN 1-56799-745-7

Editor: Susan Lauzau
Art Director: Jeff Batzli
Designer: Jennifer Markson
Photography Editor: Valerie E. Kennedy

Color separations by Fine Arts Repro House Co., Ltd.
Printed in Hong Kong by Midas Printing, Ltd.
1 3 5 7 9 10 8 6 4 2

For bulk purchases and special sales, please contact:
Friedman/Fairfax Publishers
Attention: Sales Department
15 West 26th Street
New York, NY 10010
212/685-6610 FAX 212/685-1307

Visit our website:
http://www.metrobooks.com

Table of Contents

INTRODUCTION

Once in a lifetime, if one is lucky, one so merges with sunlight and air and running water that whole eons, the eons that mountains and deserts know, might pass in a single afternoon....
—Loren Eiseley

Water in a garden always transforms it for the better, adding welcome notes of style, whimsy, solace, and magic. When the water is in motion, as with a fountain or cascade, the scene is alive and mesmerizing. And your sense of hearing—not usually awakened in a garden—is courted by the musical dance of water on water. On sunny days, droplets shimmer or glisten, playing with light in ways no plant or other object in your garden ever does. There is simply nothing quite like a fountain, and once you have installed one, you and everyone who visits will be completely captivated.

Any garden, from a formal estate to a modest suburban backyard, will benefit from a bubbling fountain. The space may be open and bright or green and shady—no matter the character of your plot, there is a suitable style for your garden. You can add a fountain to a planned pool, or with a little more effort, install one in or next to an already-present pool—in either case taking the display a step beyond the ordinary. Or consider clearing a space in a dull corner or other humdrum spot that until now has stymied your efforts to bring excitement or character. Your fountain can be the garden's focal point or it can be a hidden surprise.

This book will give you a tour of the range of fountains possible and show you how others have incorporated theirs into garden settings. Now you can dream of what your fountain will look like, what it will sound like, and how it will fit into the garden you already have or the one that you are currently composing.

So dream away, make your choice, and once your fountain is in place—relax at its side. For flowing water has the singular ability to envelop your senses, excluding all worries and cares; there is no sense of being confined, even in the smallest, tucked-away oasis or grotto. Fountains whisper, murmur, or exult, but their liberating, eternal message is a celebration of the life-giving force of water—truly, a waking dream.

ABOVE: Dome-shaped fountains are ideal for small spaces because the water's domain is so discrete and compact. Yet you still get the wonderful splashing sounds that make fountains such a joyful garden ornament.

OPPOSITE: The best fountains are in scale with their surroundings. Here, a tiny fountain gushing forth near a lilypad peeks out from a diminutive sunken tub, proof that even the most limited space can generate the bewitching sight and sound of splashing water.

LEFT: Taking a cue from European street fountains, this ingenious design combines a rock wall resembling the ramparts of a fine old castle with regularly spaced falling streams. The result is stylized yet utterly enchanting.

OPPOSITE: Matching the fountain, or fountains, to adjacent architecture is an exciting idea; the juxtaposition of static structure (in this case, the arched windows to the side and rear) and moving water creates a garden picture that resonates. The visitor might not notice right away if standing at a different vantage point, so make the best viewing spot obvious and accessible.

LEFT: Had this Italian fountain, composed of classical statuary and arcing jets, been placed in a less secluded spot, the appealing sense of intimacy would have been lost. To emulate this design, set a statuary fountain in a spot where it will be framed against an evocative background. If you can't manage a verdant grotto, a backdrop of rocks or even a fence can render a similar effect.

OPPOSITE: A trickle of water trails from a seashell into a little pool of stones; the concentration that the statue of the young woman brings to her task tends to mesmerize her audience as well. This unorthodox style of fountain is well-suited to a small garden or patio area, where the sculpture can be tucked into a pleasant spot, as if it is merely a regular visitor to the garden.

ABOVE: A sculpted basin is a classic choice for a formal landscape. In addition to the tinkling jet of water in the top, this fountain adds the surprise of spouting lions below. The artful show is achieved with concealed piping and underwater pump.

OPPOSITE: Owners of small gardens are often advised to "go up" by adding trellises or vines along walls and fences. But a wall fountain might be the most irresistible option—the necessary plumbing hardware and basin can easily be hidden from view. And the pool into which the water spills from the mounted face (or any other statuary of your choosing) need not be especially wide or long to accommodate its captivating stream of water.

ABOVE: Natural materials like this jumble of rocks and small boulders are ideal spillways. Careful placement will control the way the water flows and falls. The sound will be most animated if you can rig it so that water descends from varying heights and some of the flows are broad while others are narrow.

RIGHT: Sculpted birds perch sweetly at the edge of a diminutive fountain, providing graceful accent to a small garden. An interesting variation on the usual fountain form, water from the shallow basin cascades in a wide stripe to the pool below.

ABOVE: Fountains can also be small and subtle, like this earthenware bowl tucked in among lush greenery. Adding the mysterious, half-submerged sculpture of a face seems to hint at a strange tale, while the array of upturned faces ranged behind furthers the intrigue. Those who happen upon this enigmatic vignette will halt in their tracks to ponder the sight.

OPPOSITE: Long a staple of Japanese-style gardens, the eternally flowing bamboo spout appears in many forms— and can easily be varied to suit your space. The basin may be a large, narrow-necked jar as shown here, which generates a deep, bass sound, or you may opt for a broader, more open bowl, with its lighter, brighter music.

ABOVE: A small pedestal fountain is the centerpiece of an all-white planting. Note that the natural clay color of the fountain is in contrast to, but not incongruous with, the garden's cool green foliage. The fountain's ivy motif links the feature subtly but firmly to the surrrounding space.

ABOVE: Spilling, splashing, spraying, and lapping, this animated fountain gains superb drama from a generous flow of water. All this is achieved with elements that are not visible to the astounded viewer—internal and underwater piping and a submerged pump. When planning something this dramatic, make sure to get a powerful pump that is equal to the job. The higher the water needs to go (the further it has to travel from the main pool), the stronger the pump must be.

ABOVE: Set within a tiny pool, this glazed ceramic urn in deep cobalt is both beautiful and eminently practicable. The small bubbler in the center of the urn offers the suggestion of a fountain without the furor of a strong jet—instead, water flows gently in concentric ripples outward and over the edge of the pot, into the surrounding pool.

Chapter One

FORMAL FOUNTAINS

*W*hen you decide to install a formal fountain, your garden gains both grandeur and serenity. This holds true no matter how large or small the garden is. Any pool can be laid out so that it is in scale with its surroundings, as can the fountain itself, whether a simple jet or fan form or a "plumbed" statue such as a pensive nymph or whimsical frog (these are available in various materials, including lead, ceramic, and cast stone). The key is to select a fountain of appropriate size and a pump of adequate strength, so that the leaping, arching, spilling, or cascading water never falls outside the pool's borders. Then, depending on the size and weight of the fountain you choose, you may also have to install it atop a solid, level platform that gives it stability.

Formal fountains range from elaborate cast-iron affairs to simpler cast stone pieces, but all have in common the impression of dignity and grace. These pieces lend the landscape a majestic touch, invoking sensations of awe with their tempered streams and stately presence.

A well-done formal fountain—one that marries the sight and sound of splashing water with a planned, geometric layout and/or statuary—is a captivating sight and a sure garden focal point. The viewer cannot resist drawing near and is permitted flights of fancy no matter how mannered the feature is. And that, truly, is the magical power of such fountains—they sing within their bounds.

OPPOSITE: Here's an interesting variation on the often-seen tiered fountain—water spouts from all sides and various levels, creating an enchanting musical dance on the surface in the main basin below. Tall, clipped standards establish a secret space, while the peaceful palette of green invites a sense of calm.

RIGHT: This lively, multi-streamed, and tiered spray is achieved using a special fountain nozzle aptly called a "flower head." The sight is magnificent, and the sound as the droplets fall on the water below is a vivacious patter.

ABOVE: Fanciful statuary with classic themes—such as this head of Poseidon, Greek god of the sea, and its attending fish—give a formal fountain an air of intrigue. The viewer becomes enthralled, imagining the stories the sculptures suggest, even as the symmetrically spilling streams captivate the other senses.

ABOVE: An unusual wrought-iron fountain—an outdoor aquarium of sorts—draws visitors to a sheltered corner of this shady garden. Although most fountains are made from stone or concrete, wrought iron is also strong and weatherproof and thus an intriguing alternative. The scale of this diminutive fountain makes it a good choice for small-space gardens or for areas where you don't want the water feature to dominate the landscape.

ABOVE: When a lush, tumbling cascade is housed in a more dignified setting, the effect is daring—even a bit rebellious. The result is a display that is exciting, bringing the garden a liberating sense of motion and spontaneity without sacrificing its conventional lines.

OPPOSITE: A lofty jet of water creates a dramatic sight, enticing visitors from a distance and inspiring awe as they approach. Set in a ring-shaped pool within a circular plaza, the shape of the fountain echoes its geometric setting. For varying heights and shapes of spray, different types of fountain nozzles are available.

ABOVE: These aptly named, evenly spaced "flower sprays" conjure up images of a neat flower bed bursting with bloom, or perhaps a stage full of synchronized ballet dancers. This idea works well in a smaller pool, too, provided its shape is geometric.

RIGHT: A strict aboveground pool of solid form and rectangular lines cries out for the lighthearted presence of a fountain. The relatively small circle of this fountain's spray leaves enough water surface to act as a reflecting pool. Make the fountain compatible with the formal scene by centering it in the middle, then enjoy its lively contribution.

ABOVE: In a garden founded on neat lines and well-tended plants, your best bet is to select a fountain with a simple profile. Anything more elaborate than this single thin jet would compromise the setting's soothing appeal and restful elegance.

OPPOSITE: It's a surprising place to find a fountain—practically overhead and spouting a generous stream from on high. The genius of this design is that the garden immediately seems both larger and more intriguing. Route the spray through an impressive piece of statuary, and you have a grand sight indeed.

LEFT: Fountains needn't always spray water aloft. Here, a conventional stone fountain brings all its benefits to the garden, but its modest downward-arching streams allow the surroundings to remain in focus for the viewer. Observe how the gentle arcs of the water echo the vaulted tunnel of golden-flowered laburnum trees overhead. Deliberate or coincidental, this juxtaposition certainly adds grace to the peaceful scene.

OPPOSITE: This detail from a fountain at the Villa Ile de France shows just how much a sculpture with a human figure can do for a formal water feature. The smiling gaze of the young woman brings a smile to our own lips, causing us to slow our steps and wonder what she is admiring. Her own reflection? The soothing water? Or the intriguing creature or structure upon which she rests? Just pondering the question is reason enough to enjoy the pause.

ABOVE: A key ingredient in small courtyard gardens is a centering fountain, which provides focus and elegant ornament. The tiered design adds height, as do the flanking trees—the result is a feeling of lavishness and expansiveness in limited space.

OPPOSITE: Influenced by the classic courtyard fountains of Moorish Spain, this diminutive example contains all the basic elements that make these pieces so enticing: beautiful, hand-painted tilework; bright colors; a kinetic geometric shape; and statuary that enhances rather than overwhelms the whole. By plumbing the sidelined creatures as well as the center fountain, the sense of perpetually supplied water adds narrative charm.

ABOVE: Known as a "flower spray" or "tiered" fountain, individual streams of water travel to varying heights, rendering a somewhat irregular spray. This popular form brings many benefits to a pool: you get to savor the tinkling music of falling water and to view the varied patterns of the droplets, all while the water below gains plenty of beneficial aeration.

ABOVE: Accompanied by a leaping fish, this "water goddess" statue presides over a small pool whose edges are lined with little individual jets that spray inward. The simple yet elegant white flowers that border the pool also compel the eye toward the middle. The result is a highly classical display that revels in its self-contained beauty.

Chapter Two

SPLASHING SPRINGS

*I*f you love the sight and sound of water, there are many ways to enjoy it in your garden without installing a feature that is formal or fancy. Casual or natural-style fountains take their inspiration more directly from nature, both in their design and in the random or spontaneous way the water flows. You can delight in anything from a bubbling spring to a shimmering cascade. When you select the source from which the water emerges, enhance the sight by choosing something made of natural materials—handsome stonework, rustic bricks, or even earthenware. The possibilities are endless and exciting.

The prettiest of such fountains are flanked by complementary landscaping. Take your cue from the springs found in nature, and let plants grow freely so that they envelop or lean over the water. If foliage trails in the water or the occasional group of fallen leaves or spent flowers eddies in the pool, let it be. If plants are growing in the water, allow them to spread as they wish and bloom profusely. There is great appeal in such unsophisticated scenes. The moving water and the lush growth will share a spirited partnership, just as nature intended.

OPPOSITE: Falling leaves, falling water—this enchanting little tiered fountain conjures an unaffected, pleasant sense of harmony with nature. The coppery color of the metal offers a further visual link with crisp autumn leaves. Encroaching herbage, while neat, is sufficiently lush enough to envelop the pool. The effect is reminiscent of a small woodland spring.

RIGHT: Tiny garden? How about a tiny fountain? The principle of "going upward when you can't go outward" is a stunning success in this ingenious display; water spills merrily down through four levels on its way into the ceramic pot. The elegant clay saucers that act as sluices are beautifully in keeping with the earthy colors and verdant greenery of this patio.

Remember, though, that all naturalistic fountains are a magical illusion, brought to life by the careful choice of materials and the appropriate pipes, pump, and, sometimes, leak-proof liners. Enlist the aid of a professional who has experience with such projects, consult with water-garden suppliers, and/or do a little homework on the technical aspects. Quality workmanship and savvy installation will result in a spot whose sight and myriad sounds you will treasure.

LEFT: Shop around and you will be enchanted by the diversity of fountain forms designed by creative sculptors. Though oversized, this realistic-looking leaf basin fits easily into a secluded nook; its tiny bubbler imparts the welcome, subtle tinkle of moving water.

OPPOSITE: In many climates, a cascade can continue to run in winter, offering pleasure to those who venture out to admire it. In winter many garden accents, hardscape elements, and water features take on a fresh beauty as they ornament the stark landscape. The continuously running water also benefits any fish or plants that may be wintering over deep below by helping to keep the water aerated and free of ice.

OPPOSITE: Asian-style gardens seem to call for more symmetry and simplicity than many fountains can supply. These humble but beautifully crafted urns fit the bill perfectly as each receives a single ribbon of water from a bamboo pipe. One set would have been an entrancing sight; the presence of three makes an even stronger impression, particularly in synchronized sound.

RIGHT: The great gardens of the Vatican in Rome include this long but simply executed series of wall fountains. Two tiers of gently pouring water create double the impact. Note that the site is thoroughly shaded by mature trees. If your own garden has such a spot and you have struggled with growing plants there, perhaps a fountain offers the perfect solution.

ABOVE: A fascinating variety of materials, from handfuls of seashells and smooth stones to stacks of salvaged bricks to highly contrived symmetrical sculptures flanking the head of the pool conspire to make a unique show. Add the sliding rills of flowing water and you have a truly artful marriage of the natural and the manmade.

ABOVE: New life for pottery—this ingenious, amusing fountain simply upends a few surplus pots. The already-present drainage holes make it simple to install the necessary fountain plumbing. Another plus: the contraption is small and can easily be tucked into a corner, where its novel presence will be exclaimed over.

RIGHT: Gossamer sheets of water glide over an elevated rocky promontory in a garden corner. The sound is gentler than a full, roaring waterfall, making for a soothing display.

ABOVE: There is a wide range of delightful creatures you might be willing to invite into your water garden—as plumbed fountains. Many emit a spray from their mouth; if you happen upon one that doesn't, such as this backward-glancing snail with watery antennae, you'll have a real conversation piece.

ABOVE: It looks natural, but this enchanting manmade waterfall brings a spontaneous beauty to a secluded nook. The trick is to install both rocks and pool securely and use a lower-strength pump so that the water spills rather than spews over the lip at the top.

ABOVE: Stonework in every aspect of this setting—the fountain, the basin, and even the surrounding patio—creates a charmingly unpretentious display. Note the way that the small faucet and its simple stream eternally splashing below are in scale with each other, making for a fountain that murmurs rather than shouts.

ABOVE: Just as the most interesting gardens combine textures as well as colors, so do intriguing fountains. The aqua patina of the botanical sculpture is lovely against the soft, aged pink of the brickwork; both materials have an appealing rough-smooth surface that invites touching.

ABOVE: A bubbler of water froths out of a rock in this pool's center, a fountain that is truly in harmony with its rock-lined perimeter. The water slides softly down the rock as it returns to the pool, thus eliminating the heavy splashing that would otherwise disturb the waterlilies and other plants growing nearby.

Chapter Three

INTEGRATING A FOUNTAIN INTO THE LANDSCAPE

No matter what sort of garden you have—large or small, sunny or shady, formal or naturalistic, busy with plants or serene in its simplicity—a fountain is an inspired addition. With careful placement, it can become a focal point that the rest of the yard flatters. Or you can tuck it into a hidden corner to create an element of mystery or surprise. Either way, the trick is to make the fountain a part of the landscape, so its charms are highlighted yet it looks like it belongs.

If you already have a garden in place and don't wish to make major adjustments to the placement of your plants, you'll need to choose a display that will be compatible in size and style to the existing garden. Perhaps all that is needed is to clear out a small area, digging up and moving only a handful of plants. Or perhaps you have a focal point of some kind that you are not happy with, such as a birdbath, sundial, or garden sculpture, and you plan to simply replace it with a water show.

It is admittedly easier to design around a fountain feature. In other words, if you can, the best approach is to select and install the fountain, then add in complementary elements such as a patio, stonework, and/or landscaping once the water feature is in place. To do this, you need a firm vision of the effect you want. Consider the size and style of your house and the expanse of the garden space, as well as your dreams for the type of fountain you'd like and, of course, the amount you can afford to spend on the total project. A plan on paper (whether a rough sketch or the contracted design of a professional landscaper) is wise. Of course, like any other garden addition, you may discover that this one has a life of its own, and inspirations for minor adjustments to the fountain or its surroundings will come easily.

OPPOSITE: Semishady gardens are naturals for fountains because the constant play of sun and shade matches the random leaping, dancing movement of the water. A jet that shoots up into the air is a wise choice because it will be most visible against the dark backdrop of nearby trees. Centered on a small peninsula that juts out from a woodland garden, this display is guaranteed to capture visitors' attention.

RIGHT: Where space is limited, small and simple designs are best. This aboveground catch basin fed by the small stream issuing from the sculpted face succeeds in bringing the sight and sound of water to a restricted space. The gardener has made the most out of this wall fountain by elevating it slightly on stones and surrounding it by a symmetrical complement of handsome plants and fencework.

ABOVE: The place where garden paths merge is a perfect setting for a water feature. Various sorts of fountains would work here, but a circular-shaped, gurgling millstone fountain filled with and flanked by smooth, round stones is an inspired choice because they further echo the shape of the clearing. The fountain's understated character helps to define the tone for this garden as a place of quiet beauty.

OPPOSITE: Larger gardens call for high drama. Here a slender but towering geyser creates a grand effect without disturbing the aquatic plants in other parts of the pool. It also works well with the garden's columnar evergreens and the weeping willows; a smaller spray would be lost in such a setting.

ABOVE: Though more modest in size than the grand fountains of European gardens, this one creates the same magnificent drama, thanks to its lushly landscaped edges and centered gushing spray. The trick is to not make the display too cluttered or complex; note that there are plenty of plants, but not a lot of different kinds.

OPPOSITE: Ebullient wildflowers and herbs are in good company with the lively tiered fountain in the background. Both seem to bounce in the breeze, and greet a sunny day with eagerness. While a lower, more natural-looking fountain might have seemed like the obvious choice in this meadow setting, the high, sparkling jets of water create a more dramatic impact.

ABOVE: Selecting a fountain that is in scale with its setting is key—remember to take into account the height of the water jets as well as the sculpture itself. This fountain, viewed from a few yards away, sprays only slightly higher than the adjacent perennials and low wall.

OPPOSITE: The elegant beauty of a single spray arching upward brings serenity and interest to a shady area. The pretty violas that ring the pool provide definition to its edges but don't steal the show. The shadows of the pool act in opposition to the shimmering light on the distant gazebo, providing a stunning contrast between these two garden elements.

ABOVE: A swimming pool with a fountain? Why not? The dancing figure and the single shooting spray both direct the eye into the inviting water surface, adding the right touch of activity to a relaxing scene.

ABOVE: This fountain at the mission in Carmel, California, provides a classic example of the Spanish style. A hexago-nal basin is centered with a bowl-shaped fountain; the edges of the basin are low and wide enough to sit on, inviting visitors to pause and contemplate the pretty garden or the water's sprinkled surface, or to trail a hand in the cooling water. The earthy color of both basin and fountain echo the hues of adobe walls and tile roof, offering a simple lesson in matching garden features to architecture.

ABOVE: Because this garden has a serene mood, and even includes a chair set out to invite rest and contemplation, a subtler fountain is a wise choice. This foaming fountain head calmly enhances the garden rather than taking the spotlight. Note that, because of the fountain's supporting role in the garden, the pool has been sited against the wall of a greenhouse rather than in the center of the lawn.

ABOVE: A long, narrow fountain display is the perfect way to introduce water to an attenuated garden space. Installing several smaller jets along the waterway keeps the eye moving and works well with the symmetrical layout of the adjacent flower borders. If there's room, an additional, aboveground fountain at the end gives the garden a dramatic destination or focal point.

ABOVE: A truly inspired designer added this unusual shallow fountain to the formal terrace. The pool has a strictly defined domain, as do the terra-cotta pots that stand in attendance. But like the lush evergreens that fill those pots, the splashing rills of water offer a measured impression of vitality, even exuberance.

Chapter Four

PLANTINGS TO ACCENT A FOUNTAIN

The most memorable fountains fit into a garden with ease because they have been flanked or surrounded by attractive, complementary landscaping. Even a small or modest-looking fountain can be greatly enhanced by well-chosen plantings; large fountains also require thoughtful plant choices. But the intent is always the same: to create an oasis, a place to pause and enjoy the sight and sound of water in the gentle company of flowers and greenery.

You may choose plants that echo or repeat the action of the water. Many plants seem to "fountain" up out of the earth, with their foliage turning outward and arching down at the tips. Notice also how many flowers surge upward. Even shrubs and trees can imitate or enhance the form of flowing water, leaning protectively over the surface. Any of these options—carefully chosen to be in scale with the fountain's form and sensitively sited—add greatly to the spot's beauty and drama.

Another approach is to plant as if you were framing a picture, which in a sense, you are. Plants of modest mounding habits are naturals for this job. Alternatively, use exclusively one plant or one color, or create a simple, repeatable pattern around the pool or basin's perimeter. Just remember that your goal is to direct attention to the water itself and especially to the activity of the flowing or spouting water.

One other way to go is to allow, or put in place, surrounding plants that make a backdrop for the play of water. Dark, dense foliage such as that of evergreens—hedges, shrubs, or trees—are ideal, as are broadleaf evergreens. Whatever plants you choose to accent your fountain, remember that the idea is to focus on the water show and let the landscaping play a supportive but secondary role.

ABOVE: Sculpture that is complex and especially striking should be enjoyed with minimal distractions, which is why this magnificent ram's head fountain is modestly flanked by nothing more than trailing ivy and green topiary. The result is a display that has an established yet intriguing air to it, as if you had stumbled upon an ancient, hidden garden.

OPPOSITE: This fan-style fountain already provides so much vertical interest that the array of low-growing, horizontally spreading plants at its feet are a welcome sight. Observe, though, how subtly but aptly the straplike foliage of a lone iris, just behind the fountain, mimics the spray's form.

ABOVE: When a garden is given over to more than one fountain, there are many landscaping opportunities. Here, the fountain composed of a stout collection of ascending basins is attended by a lush assortment of taller bloomers, giving it weight and majesty. Meanwhile, the slim, tall spray to the left is not encroached upon by the landscaping, so it can play freely out in the open.

ABOVE: Bright flowers gather at the base of this lovely, single-jet fountain, delighting the eye even as they direct attention to what is above and ahead. The dark foliage behind the fountain makes an ideal backdrop for the water stream.

ABOVE: This Japanese-style fountain combines the refined form of urn-shaped bowls with a traditional bamboo spout that gently and perpetually spills water. By placing the feature facing outward from the base of a slope, and by choosing plants with cascading habits, the direction of the flow of the water seems natural, indeed inevitable.

OPPOSITE: In a densely planted area, a tall, flashy fountain would not only look out of place, it would probably hinder the healthy growth of these lovers of still water. The solution? Install a foaming fountain head, which makes splendid musical sounds but keeps splashing within a discrete area. A base of stones around the water further limits disturbances.

RIGHT: Simplicity rules in this shady nook, where a single ribbon of water is delivered to a small trough. Brightness is injected not only by the merry sound but by a bit of variegated foliage (the hosta, the iris spears) and a white calla lily.

OPPOSITE TOP: Water is cooling. So is shade. The perfect marriage occurs in a modest formal fountain under a canopy of established trees. The small basin is rimmed only by a monochromatic color scheme provided by shade-loving, profuse-blooming tuberous begonias.

OPPOSITE BOTTOM: In a big pool occupied by a variety of aquatic plants, this rushing, spilling spray occupies a central spot. Here its flow does not disturb the motion-sensitive lilypads. Notice also how the clump-forming blooming flowers such as canna occupy about the same amount of surface space as the fountain and its stone—this way they don't crowd it or unduly divert our attention.

ABOVE: Why not create a grotto in your garden, with all the secret, splashing lushness that the feature implies? Here, a small pool has been tucked into a corner and surrounded by generous foliage plants, especially lush clumps of ferns, which adore such damp, shady conditions.

OPPOSITE: Carefully chosen statuary, such as an attentive nymph, and a handful of lush "fountain-form" plants help make a water feature its own charming little world. Ornamental grasses, like these green and gold specimens, are favorite pairings for fountains. With the right balance of materials and plants, you can create a magical haven to which you can retreat and let your imagination wander.

ABOVE: Unusual fountains call for dramatic landscaping that complements but doesn't usurp the scene. The above-ground pool and surrounding brick walk give this elaborate fountain all the room it needs; exciting, bright flowers beyond that boundary, such as long-blooming rudbeckias, help set the lively tone.

ABOVE: Here, well-chosen flowers enhance the diminutive fountain display—the lilies, especially, echo the spray's profile. A plus: lilies are generally long bloomers, so the display can be enjoyed for weeks on end.

INDEX

PHOTO CREDITS